# fast & simple

## a visual step-by-step guide to perfect cooking

LOVE FOOD™

This edition published in 2012
LOVE FOOD is an imprint of Parragon Books Ltd

Parragon
Queen Street House
4 Queen Street
Bath BA1 1HE, UK

www.parragon.com

ISBN: 978-1-4454-7864-7

Printed in China

Additional photography by Mike Cooper
Introduction by Linda Doeser
New recipes by Christine France
Photography by Mike Cooper
Home economy by Lincoln Jefferson

Notes for the Reader
This book uses standard kitchen measuring spoons and cups. All spoon and cup measurements
are level unless otherwise indicated. Unless otherwise stated, milk is assumed to be whole, eggs
are large, individual vegetables are medium, and pepper is freshly ground black pepper. Unless
otherwise stated, all root vegetables should be washed and peeled before using. Garnishes and
serving suggestions are all optional and not necessarily included in the recipe ingredients or method.

The times given are only an approximate guide. Preparation times differ according to the techniques
used by different people and the cooking times may also vary from those given. Optional ingredients,
variations, or serving suggestions have not been included in the calculations.

Recipes using raw or very lightly cooked eggs should be avoided by infants, the elderly, pregnant
women, and anyone with a chronic illness. Pregnant and breast-feeding women are advised to avoid
eating peanuts and peanut products. People with nut allergies should be aware that some of the
prepared ingredients used in the recipes in this book may contain nuts. Always check the packaging
before use.

Vegetarians should be aware that some of the prepared ingredients used in the recipes in this book
may contain animal products. Always check the package before use.

# contents

# introduction

**This wonderful cookbook, with its wealth of stunning and particularly useful photographs, will be an invaluable addition to any cook's bookshelf. The recipes are clear, easy to follow, beautifully illustrated and temptingly tasty, so whatever your level of expertise in the kitchen, you are virtually guaranteed success every time.**

Every recipe starts with a photograph of all the ingredients, but this is more than just a pretty picture or—even less helpful—a montage that is not to scale, so that a chile appears to be the same size as a whole fish. Instead, it serves as a handy way to check that you have everything ready before you start cooking. Just comparing the picture with the ingredients arranged on your own countertop or kitchen table will make sure that you haven't forgotten anything and, when it's time to add the garlic, for example, you have already chopped it as specified in the ingredients list. If you're uncertain about how small to dice fruit or how finely to crush cookies, a glance at the photograph will provide an instant answer.

Each short and straightforward step of the method is clearly explained, without any jargon or difficult technical terms. Once again, what you see in the photograph is what you should expect to see in front of you. Not only is this reassuring for the novice cook, but those with more experience will find it a helpful reminder of the little touches that can easily be overlooked. Each recipe has a wonderful photograph of the finished dish, complete with any serving suggestions.

## why you need this book

Eating well is one of the primary keys to good health for you and your family, yet the pace of modern life is often frantic and time is limited. Few people have the time to spend hours in the kitchen and, equally important, no one wants to struggle trying to understand a complicated recipe that turns out to be disappointing and not what was expected.

In this book there are easy recipes for delicious dishes for all occasions and every taste, from succulent stir-fried beef to elegant glazed duck and from spicy seafood stew to great vegetarian casseroles, and there is also a chapter of wonderfully self-indulgent desserts. All of the recipes take less than half an hour to prepare, and many can be made in just minutes.

## hints and tips for quick cooking

- Read all the way through the recipe—both the ingredients list and method—before you start, so that you know exactly what you will need. Scrabbling about at the back of the pantry to find a rarely used ingredient or moving half a dozen other utensils to reach the one you need in the middle of cooking a dish is, at best, exasperating and, at worst, liable to cause the dish you are cooking to burn.

- As you finish using utensils, move them out of your way. A cluttered counter is the enemy of speed and efficiency, and can be dangerous.

- Collect together all your ingredients and make sure that they are ready to use— for example, vegetables peeled or washed. In addition, do any initial preparation described in the ingredients list, such as chopping onions. Check the photograph for comparison.

- Ovens and broilers take time to heat up, so turn them on as soon as you go into the kitchen. Convection ovens do not usually require preheating, but conventional ovens can take 15 minutes to reach the specified temperature.

- Be realistic about how much time you have and what you can reasonably handle. There's no point in cooking the main course in a few minutes if the vegetables you intend to accompany it will take a lot longer. Consider a no-cook dessert or an appetizer that can be prepared in advance if the main course requires your undivided attention.

- Arrange the plates and bowls of ingredients in the order in which they will be used. If a number of ingredients, such as flavorings and spices, will be added at the same time, put them in small piles on the same plate.

## time-saving shortcuts

- Not all vegetables have to be peeled before cooking. Most of the nutrients are often found just under the skin, so it is better to simply scrub them. Thin-skinned vegetables, such as zucchini and eggplants, do not need peeling. However, "old" vegetables should always be peeled, and so too should carrots, because they can retain chemicals beneath the skin.

- The easiest way to peel tomatoes, nectarines, peaches, and shallots is to put them into a heatproof bowl and pour in boiling water to cover. Let stand for 30–60 seconds, then drain. The skins will slip off much more easily.

- To peel a garlic clove, lightly crush it by pressing down with the flat blade of a chef's knife. The skin can then be removed easily and the garlic can be chopped, sliced or, quickest of all, crushed with a garlic press.

- Some ingredients—for example, ham, some fresh herbs, and dried fruit—are much easier and quicker to snip into pieces with scissors instead of dicing with a knife. Trim green beans and snow peas with kitchen scissors, too.

- If you have any leftover fresh bread crumbs or shredded cheese, divide into portions and freeze for another day. They make the perfect quick topping for gratins or casseroles.

- Don't waste time peeling avocados if you will be mashing or processing the flesh. Simply halve and pit, then scoop out the flesh with a spoon.

- When using the food processor to chop vegetables, such as onions, make extra and store in sealed plastic food bags in the refrigerator, ready to use as and when you need them during the week.

7

- To seed peppers, halve them lengthwise and cut out the membranes, together with most of the seeds, with a small knife. Turn the halves over and tap sharply on a cutting board so that any remaining seeds fall out.

- Melt chocolate in the microwave oven. Break it into pieces and put it into a microwave-proof bowl. Heat on MEDIUM for 10 seconds, then stir. Return to the microwave and heat for another 10 seconds before checking and stirring again—even when it's melted, it will hold its shape, so you cannot tell if it's ready just by looking at it. Melt white chocolate on LOW.

- To coat cubes of meat in flour before browning, put the flour into a plastic food bag and add the cubes a few at a time. Hold the bag closed and shake gently until the meat is coated. Repeat until finished.

- Leftover wine can also be frozen. Freeze it in an ice-cube tray, and the next time you're cooking a casserole, you can add a cube or two to add extra depth of flavor.

- When slicing soft cheese, such as Camembert, dampen the blade of the knife to prevent the slices from sticking to it.

- Take advantage of convenience foods, such as bags of diced vegetables, washed salad greens, prepared sauces and condiments, canned beans and tomatoes, and jars of chopped garlic, ginger, and chiles. Strike a balance between cost and saving time.

# meat & poultry

grilled steak with hot chile salsa 11
teriyaki steak 13
paprika steak wraps with horseradish cream 15
hot sesame beef 17
chorizo, chile & chickpea casserole 19
pork & rosemary burgers 21
pork in plum sauce 23
orange & lemon crispy lamb cutlets 25
baked tapenade chicken 27
chicken with creamy penne 29
creamy turkey & broccoli gnocchi 31
turkey cutlets with prosciutto & sage 33
duck breasts with citrus glaze 35

# grilled steak with hot chile salsa

**serves 4**

### ingredients

sunflower oil, for brushing
4 tenderloin steaks, about
  8 ounces each
salt and pepper
mâche, to garnish

### hot chile salsa

4 fresh red habanero chiles
4 fresh green poblano chiles
3 tomatoes, peeled, seeded,
  and diced
2 tablespoons chopped cilantro

1 tablespoon red wine vinegar
2 tablespoons olive oil
salt

**>1** For the salsa, preheat the broiler to high. Arrange the chiles on an aluminum foil-lined broiler rack and cook under the preheated broiler, turning frequently, until blackened and charred.

**>2** Let the chiles cool. When cool enough to handle, peel off and discard the skins. Halve and seed the chiles, then finely chop the flesh. Mix together the chiles, tomatoes, and cilantro in a bowl.

**>3** Mix together the vinegar and olive oil in a small bowl. Season with salt and pour over the salsa. Toss well, cover, and chill until required.

**>4** Heat a ridged grill pan over medium heat and brush with the oil. Season the steaks with salt and pepper, and cook for 2–4 minutes on each side, or until cooked to your liking. Serve immediately with the salsa, garnished with mâche.

# teriyaki steak

**serves 4**

## ingredients

4 tenderloin steaks, about
  6 ounces each
2 tablespoons vegetable oil
2 cups fresh bean sprouts

4 scallions, trimmed
  and thinly sliced
salt and pepper

## teriyaki sauce

2 tablespoons mirin
  (Japanese rice wine)
2 tablespoons sake or
  pale dry sherry
¼ cup dark soy sauce
1 teaspoon sugar

**>1** Season the steaks with salt and pepper and set aside.

**>2** For the sauce, combine the mirin, sake, soy sauce, and sugar in a bowl, stirring well.

**>3** Heat 1 tablespoon of the oil in a skillet over high heat. Add the bean sprouts and cook quickly, tossing in the hot oil for 30 seconds.

**>4** Remove from the skillet and drain on paper towels.

**>5** Add the remaining oil to the skillet and, when hot, add the steaks. Cook for 1–3 minutes on each side, or until cooked to your liking. Remove from the skillet and keep warm. Remove the skillet from the heat.

**>6** Add the sauce and scallions to the skillet, return to the heat, and simmer for 2 minutes, stirring until the sauce thickens. Divide the sprouts among four plates, top with a steak, and spoon the scallions and sauce over them.

# paprika steak wraps with horseradish cream

serves 4

## ingredients

4 tenderloin steaks, about
   6 ounces each
1 garlic clove, crushed
2 teaspoons smoked paprika,
   plus extra for sprinkling

sunflower oil, for brushing
½ cup crème fraîche
3 tablespoons creamed
   horseradish
8 small flour tortillas

4 cups arugula
2 firm, ripe avocados, peeled,
   pitted, and sliced
1 red onion, thinly sliced
salt and pepper

**>1** Rub the steaks with the garlic and sprinkle both sides with the paprika. Season with salt and pepper.

**>2** Heat a ridged grill pan over high heat and brush with the oil. Add the steaks and cook for 6–8 minutes, turning once. Remove from the heat and let rest for 5 minutes.

**>3** Mix together the crème fraîche and horseradish, then spread half over the tortillas.

**>4** Slice the steaks into strips. Divide among the tortillas with the arugula, avocado, and red onion, wrapping the sides over. Serve the wraps with a spoonful of horseradish cream, sprinkled with paprika.

# hot sesame beef

serves 4

## ingredients

1 pound tenderloin steak, cut into thin strips

1½ tablespoons sesame seeds

½ cup beef stock

2 tablespoons soy sauce

2 tablespoons grated fresh ginger

2 garlic cloves, finely chopped

1 teaspoon cornstarch

½ teaspoon crushed red pepper

3 tablespoons sesame oil

1 large head of broccoli, cut into florets

1 yellow bell pepper, seeded and thinly sliced

1 fresh red chile, thinly sliced

1 tablespoon chili oil, or to taste

salt and pepper

1 tablespoon chopped fresh cilantro, to garnish

cooked wild rice, to serve

**>1** Mix the beef strips with 1 tablespoon of the sesame seeds in a small bowl. In a separate bowl, stir together the stock, soy sauce, ginger, garlic, cornstarch, and crushed red pepper.

**>2** Heat 1 tablespoon of the sesame oil in a large wok. Stir-fry the beef strips for 2–3 minutes. Remove and set aside, then wipe the wok with paper towels.

**>3** Heat the remaining sesame oil in the wok, add the broccoli, yellow bell pepper, red chile, and chili oil, and stir-fry for 2–3 minutes. Stir in the stock mixture, cover, and simmer for 2 minutes.

**>4** Return the beef to the wok and simmer until the juices thicken, stirring occasionally. Cook for an additional 1–2 minutes. Sprinkle with the remaining sesame seeds and season with salt and pepper. Serve over wild rice and garnish with fresh cilantro.

# chorizo, chile & chickpea casserole

serves 4

## ingredients

2 tablespoons olive oil

1 onion, sliced

1 large yellow bell pepper, seeded and sliced

1 garlic clove, crushed

1 teaspoon crushed red pepper

8 ounces chorizo sausage

1 (14½-ounce) can chopped tomatoes

1 (15–16 ounce) can chickpeas, drained

1 cup long-grain rice

handful of arugula

salt and pepper

¼ cup coarsely chopped fresh basil, to garnish

>1 Heat the oil in a flameproof casserole dish and sauté the onion over medium heat, stirring occasionally, for 5 minutes.

>2 Add the yellow bell pepper, garlic, and crushed red pepper and cook for 2 minutes, stirring.

>3 Chop the chorizo into bite-size chunks and stir into the casserole.

>4 Add the tomatoes and chickpeas and season with salt and pepper. Bring to a boil, cover, and simmer for 10 minutes.

>5 Meanwhile, cook the rice in a saucepan of lightly salted boiling water for 10–12 minutes, until tender. Drain.

>6 Stir the arugula into the casserole. Serve spooned over the rice, garnished with chopped basil.

# pork & rosemary burgers

**serves 4**

## ingredients

1 pound fresh ground pork

1 small onion, finely chopped

1 garlic clove, crushed

1 tablespoon finely chopped fresh
  rosemary

sunflower oil, for brushing

1 small French baguette,
  split and cut into four

2 tomatoes, sliced

4 pickles, sliced

¼ cup Greek-style yogurt

2 tablespoons chopped fresh mint

salt and pepper

> **>1** Use your hands to mix together the pork, onion, garlic, and rosemary, seasoned with salt and pepper.

> **>2** Divide the mixture into four balls and shape into flat patties.

> **>3** Brush a ridged grill pan or skillet with the oil and cook the patties over medium heat for 6–8 minutes, turning once, until golden and cooked through.

> **>4** Place a burger on the bottom half of each piece of baguette and top with the tomatoes and pickles. Mix together the yogurt and mint. Spoon the minty yogurt over the burgers and replace the baguette tops to serve.

# pork in plum sauce

serves 4

## ingredients

1¼ pounds pork tenderloin
2 tablespoons peanut oil
1 orange bell pepper, seeded
   and sliced
1 bunch scallions, sliced

8 ounces oyster mushrooms, sliced
3 cups fresh bean sprouts
2 tablespoons dry sherry
⅔ cup plum sauce

8 ounces medium egg noodles
salt and pepper
chopped fresh cilantro,
   to garnish

**>1** Slice the pork into long, thin strips.

**>2** Heat the oil in a wok and stir-fry the pork for 2–3 minutes.

**>3** Add the bell pepper and stir-fry for 2 minutes, then add the scallions, mushrooms, and bean sprouts.

**>4** Stir-fry for 2–3 minutes, then add the sherry and plum sauce and heat until boiling. Season well with salt and pepper.

**>5** Meanwhile, cook the noodles in a saucepan of lightly salted boiling water for 4 minutes, or according to the package directions, until tender.

**>6** Drain the noodles, then add to the wok and toss well. Serve immediately, garnished with chopped cilantro.

# orange & lemon crispy lamb cutlets

**serves 2**

## ingredients

1 garlic clove, crushed

1 tablespoon olive oil

2 tablespoons finely grated orange rind

2 tablespoons finely grated lemon rind

6 lamb cutlets

salt and pepper

orange wedges, to serve

**>1** Preheat a ridged grill pan.

**>2** Mix together the garlic, oil, and citrus rinds in a bowl. Season with salt and pepper.

**>3** Brush the mixture over the lamb cutlets, covering both sides.

**>4** Cook the cutlets in the preheated grill pan for 4–5 minutes on each side. Serve immediately with orange wedges for squeezing over.

# baked tapenade chicken

serves 4

## ingredients

4 skinless, boneless chicken breasts
¼ cup green olive tapenade
8 thin slices pancetta
2 garlic cloves, chopped

16 cherry tomatoes, halved
½ cup dry white wine
2 tablespoons olive oil

8 slices ciabatta
salt and pepper

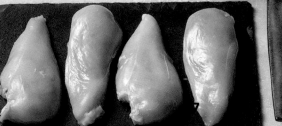

**>1** Preheat the oven to 425°F. Place the chicken breasts on a cutting board and cut three deep slashes into each.

**>2** Spread a tablespoon of the tapenade over each chicken breast, pushing it into the slashes with a spatula. Wrap each chicken breast in two slices of pancetta.

**>3** Place the chicken breasts in a shallow ovenproof dish and arrange the garlic and tomatoes around them.

**>4** Season with salt and pepper, then pour the wine and 1 tablespoon of the oil over them.

**>5** Bake in the preheated oven for about 20 minutes, until the juices run clear when the chicken is pierced with a skewer or the tip of a sharp knife. Cover the dish with aluminum foil and let stand for 5 minutes.

**>6** Meanwhile, preheat the broiler to high. Brush the ciabatta with the remaining oil and cook under the preheated broiler for 2–3 minutes, turning once, until golden. Serve with the toasted ciabatta.

# chicken with creamy penne

**serves 2**

## ingredients

8 ounces dried penne

1 tablespoon olive oil

2 skinless, boneless chicken breasts

¼ cup dry white wine

¾ cup frozen peas

½ cup heavy cream

salt

¼–⅓ cup chopped fresh flat-leaf parsley, to garnish

**>1** Bring a large saucepan of lightly salted water to a boil. Add the pasta and cook for about 8–10 minutes, or according to the package directions, until tender but still firm to the bite.

**>2** Meanwhile, heat the oil in a skillet, add the chicken, and cook over medium heat for about 4 minutes on each side.

**>3** Pour in the wine and cook over high heat until it has almost evaporated.

**>4** Drain the pasta. Add the peas, cream, and pasta to the skillet and stir well. Cover and simmer for 2 minutes. Garnish with chopped parsley and serve.

# creamy turkey & broccoli gnocchi

**serves 4**

## ingredients

1 tablespoon sunflower oil

1 pound turkey stir-fry strips

2 small leeks, sliced diagonally

1 pound store-bought
  fresh gnocchi

3 cups broccoli florets

⅓ cup crème fraîche or
  sour cream

1 tablespoon whole-grain mustard

3 tablespoons orange juice

salt and pepper

3 tablespoons toasted pine nuts,
  to serve

**>1** Heat the oil in a wok or large skillet, then add the turkey and leeks and stir-fry over high heat for 5–6 minutes.

**>2** Meanwhile, bring a saucepan of lightly salted water to a boil. Add the gnocchi and broccoli, then cook for 3–4 minutes.

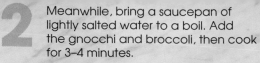

**>3** Drain the gnocchi and broccoli and stir into the turkey mixture.

**>4** Mix together the crème fraîche, mustard, and orange juice in a small bowl. Season with salt and pepper, then stir into the wok. Serve immediately, sprinkled with pine nuts.

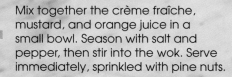

# turkey cutlets with prosciutto & sage

**serves 2**

## ingredients

2 skinless, boneless turkey cutlets

2 slices prosciutto, halved

4 fresh sage leaves

2 tablespoons all-purpose flour

2 tablespoons olive oil

1 tablespoon butter

salt and pepper

lemon wedges, to serve

**>1** Slice each turkey cutlet in half horizontally into two thinner pieces.

**>2** Put each piece between two sheets of plastic wrap and pound lightly with a rolling pin. Season each piece of turkey with salt and pepper.

**>3** Lay half a slice of ham on each piece of turkey, put a sage leaf on top, and secure with a toothpick.

**>4** Mix the flour with salt and pepper on a large plate. Dust both sides of each piece of turkey with the seasoned flour.

**>5** Heat the oil in a large skillet, add the butter, and cook until foaming. Add the pieces of turkey and cook over medium heat for 1½ minutes, sage-side down.

**>6** Turn the turkey over and cook for an additional 30 seconds, or until golden brown and cooked through. Serve immediately with lemon wedges for squeezing over.

# duck breasts with citrus glaze

**serves 4**

## ingredients

¼ cup packed light brown sugar
finely grated rind and juice of
  1 orange
finely grated rind and juice of
  1 large lemon

finely grated rind and juice of
  1 lime
4 duck breasts, skin on
2 tablespoons olive oil
salt and pepper

freshly cooked sugar snap peas
  and orange wedges,  to serve

**>1** Put the sugar in a small saucepan, add just enough water to cover, and heat gently until dissolved.

**>2** Add the citrus rinds and juices and bring to a boil.

**>3** Reduce the heat and simmer for about 10 minutes, until syrupy. Remove from the heat.

**>4** Meanwhile, score the skin of the duck breasts with a sharp knife in a crisscross pattern and rub with salt and pepper.

**>5** Heat the oil in a skillet. Place the duck breasts skin-side down in the skillet and cook for 5 minutes on each side, until the flesh is just pink. Keep warm.

**>6** Slice the duck breasts and transfer to warm plates. Arrange some sugar snap peas on each plate, spoon over the glaze, and serve immediately, with orange wedges for squeezing over the duck.

# fish & seafood

seared sesame salmon with bok choy 39
quick & creamy fish gratin 41
peppered tuna steaks 43
fish sticks with chili mayonnaise 45
sea bass with olive gremolata 47
speedy tuna pizza 49
hot smoked salmon on hash browns 51
spicy thai seafood stew 53
calamari with shrimp & fava beans 55
monkfish with a lemon & parsley crust 57
thai shrimp noodle bowl 59
wine-steamed mussels 61

# seared sesame salmon with bok choy

serves 4

## ingredients

1-inch piece fresh ginger
1 tablespoon soy sauce
1 teaspoon sesame oil

4 skinless salmon fillets
2 tablespoons sesame seeds
lime wedges, to serve

## stir-fry

2 small bok choy
1 bunch scallions
1 tablespoon sunflower oil
1 teaspoon sesame oil
salt and pepper

**>1** Peel and finely grate the ginger and mix with the soy sauce and sesame oil in a shallow dish. Add the salmon fillets, turning to coat evenly on both sides.

**>2** Sprinkle the salmon on one side with half the sesame seeds, then turn and sprinkle the other side with the remaining sesame seeds.

**>3** Cut the bok choy lengthwise into quarters. Cut the scallions into thick diagonal slices.

**>4** Preheat a heavy skillet. Add the salmon and cook for 3–4 minutes. Turn and cook for an additional 3–4 minutes.

**>5** Meanwhile, heat the sunflower oil and sesame oil in a wok, add the bok choy and scallions, and stir-fry for 2–3 minutes. Season with salt and pepper.

**>6** Divide the vegetables among warm serving plates and place the salmon on top. Serve immediately with lime wedges for squeezing over the fish.

# quick & creamy fish gratin

**serves 4**

## ingredients

1 tablespoon olive oil

2 shallots, finely chopped

⅔ cup dry white wine

1 bay leaf

3 cups thickly sliced, white button mushrooms

⅓ cup crème fraîche

1 pound firm white fish fillets, such as cod or flounder, cut into chunks

6 ounces cooked, peeled shrimp

1¼ cups frozen peas

3 tablespoons butter

3 cups fresh white bread crumbs

salt and pepper

chopped fresh flat-leaf parsley, to garnish

**>1** Heat the oil in an ovenproof saucepan or a shallow flameproof casserole dish and sauté the shallots for 2–3 minutes, until softened.

**>2** Add the wine, bay leaf, and mushrooms and simmer for 2 minutes, stirring occasionally.

**>3** Stir in the crème fraîche and add the fish. Season with salt and pepper. Bring to a boil, cover, and simmer for 5–6 minutes, until the fish is almost cooked.

**>4** Remove and discard the bay leaf, then add the shrimp and peas and bring back to a boil.

**>5** Meanwhile, melt the butter in a separate saucepan and stir in the bread crumbs. Preheat the broiler to medium. Spread the bread crumb mixture evenly over the top of the fish mixture.

**>6** Place the saucepan under the preheated broiler for 3–4 minutes, until the topping is golden brown and bubbling. Sprinkle with chopped parsley and serve hot.

# peppered
# tuna steaks

serves 4

## ingredients

4 tuna steaks, about
   6 ounces each
4 teaspoons sunflower oil
   or olive oil

1 teaspoon salt
2 tablespoons pink, green, and
   black peppercorns, coarsely
   crushed

handful of fresh arugula,
   to garnish
lemon wedges, to serve

## >1

Brush the tuna steaks with the oil.

## >2

Sprinkle with the salt.

## >3

Coat the fish in the crushed peppercorns.

## >4

Heat a ridged grill pan over medium heat. Add the tuna and cook for 2–3 minutes on each side. Garnish with arugula and serve with lemon wedges for squeezing over the fish.

# fish sticks with chili mayonnaise

**serves 4**

## ingredients

1⅔ cups all-purpose flour
3 eggs
1¼ cups matzo meal
1 pound firm white fish fillets, such
  as cod or flounder, cut into strips

sunflower oil or peanut oil,
  for shallow-frying
salt and pepper

### chili mayonnaise

2 tablespoons sweet chili sauce
¼–⅓ cup mayonnaise

>1 Mix the flour with plenty of salt and pepper on a large flat plate.

>2 Beat the eggs in a bowl.

>3 Spread out the matzo meal on another flat plate.

>4 Dip the fish pieces into the seasoned flour, then into the beaten egg, then into the matzo meal, making sure the pieces are coated well.

>5 Pour the oil into a nonstick skillet to a depth of ½ inch and heat. Cook the fish pieces in batches for a few minutes, turning once, until golden brown and cooked through.

>6 For the chili mayonnaise, put the chili sauce and mayonnaise in a bowl. Mix together until combined. Transfer the fish to warm plates and serve with the chili mayonnaise on the side.

# sea bass with olive gremolata

**serves 4**

## ingredients

2 pounds small new potatoes

4 sea bass fillets, about
  6 ounces each

1 tablespoon olive oil

¼ cup dry white wine

salt and pepper

lemon wedges, to serve

## olive gremolata

grated rind of 1 lemon

1 garlic clove, chopped

2 large handfuls flat-leaf parsley

¾ cup pitted ripe black olives

2 tablespoons capers

2 tablespoons olive oil

**>1** Cook the potatoes in a saucepan of lightly salted, boiling water for 15–20 minutes, or until tender.

**>2** Meanwhile, make the gremolata. Place the lemon rind, garlic, parsley, olives, capers, and oil in a food processor and process briefly to form a coarse paste.

**>3** Brush the sea bass with the oil and season with salt and pepper. Heat a heavy skillet and cook the sea bass for 5–6 minutes, turning once.

**>4** Remove the fish from the skillet and keep warm. Stir the wine into the skillet and boil for 1 minute, stirring.

**>5** Add the gremolata to the skillet and stir for a few seconds to heat gently.

**>6** Drain the potatoes and crush lightly with a wooden spoon or potato masher. Serve the sea bass and crushed potatoes topped with the gremolata, with lemon wedges for squeezing over the fish.

# speedy tuna
# pizza
**serves 4**

## ingredients

3 tablespoons red pesto

1 (12-inch) store-bought pizza crust

1 (5 ounce) can tuna in sunflower
   oil, drained

12 cherry tomatoes, halved

1 cup diced mozzarella cheese,

2 tablespoons capers

8 small ripe black olives, pitted

1 tablespoon olive oil

salt and pepper

**1** Preheat the oven to 425°F. Spread the pesto evenly over the pizza crust.

**2** Coarsely flake the tuna and arrange over the pizza.

**3** Scatter the tomatoes, mozzarella, capers, and olives over the pizza. Season with salt and pepper.

**4** Drizzle the oil over the pizza and bake in the preheated oven for about 15 minutes, or until golden and bubbling. Serve the pizza hot or cold.

# hot smoked salmon on hash browns

serves 4

## ingredients

7 potatoes, such as russets or white
  rounders (about 1¾ pounds)

1 onion

2 tablespoons chopped fresh dill,
  plus extra sprigs to garnish

1 teaspoon celery salt

2 tablespoons butter

2 tablespoons olive oil

1 bunch watercress

1 tablespoon walnut oil

2 tablespoons lemon juice

8 ounces hot smoked salmon,
  coarsely flaked

pepper

lemon wedges, to serve

**>1** Grate the potatoes and onion in a food processor. Transfer to a clean dish towel and squeeze out as much moisture as possible.

**>2** Stir in the chopped dill and celery salt and season well with pepper. Divide into eight portions.

**>3** Heat half the butter and oil in a large skillet. Add four mounds of the potato mixture and flatten lightly. Cook for 4–5 minutes, until golden underneath.

**>4** Flip the hash browns over to cook on the other side until golden brown. Remove from the skillet and keep warm while you repeat with the remaining mixture.

**>5** Toss the watercress with the walnut oil and 1 tablespoon of the lemon juice. Divide among the serving plates and place the hash browns on top.

**>6** Top with the salmon, sprinkle with the remaining lemon juice, and season with pepper. Garnish with dill sprigs and serve with lemon wedges for squeezing over the fish.

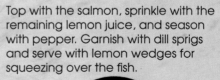

# spicy thai seafood stew

**serves 4**

## ingredients

8 ounces squid, cleaned and
  tentacles discarded
1 pound firm fish fillets, preferably
  monkfish or red snapper
1 tablespoon corn oil
4 shallots, finely chopped
2 garlic cloves, finely chopped

2 tablespoons Thai green
  curry paste
2 small lemongrass stems, finely
  chopped
1 teaspoon shrimp paste
2 cups coconut milk

8 ounces jumbo shrimp, peeled
  and deveined
12 clams, scrubbed
8 fresh basil leaves, chopped,
  plus extra leaves to garnish
freshly cooked rice, to serve

**>1** Using a sharp knife, cut the squid into thick rings and cut the fish into bite-size chunks.

**>2** Preheat a large wok, then add the oil and heat. Add the shallots, garlic, and curry paste and stir-fry for 1–2 minutes.

**>3** Add the lemongrass and shrimp paste, then stir in the coconut milk and bring to a boil.

**>4** Reduce the heat until the liquid is simmering gently, then add the squid, fish, and shrimp and simmer for 2 minutes.

**>5** Discard any clams with broken shells and any that refuse to close when tapped. Add the clams and simmer for an additional minute, or until the clams have opened. Discard any that remain closed.

**>6** Sprinkle the chopped basil over the stew. Transfer to serving plates, garnish with basil leaves, and serve immediately with freshly cooked rice.

# calamari with shrimp & fava beans

serves 4–6

## ingredients

2 tablespoons olive oil

4 scallions, thinly sliced

2 garlic cloves, finely chopped

1 pound cleaned squid bodies, thickly sliced

½ cup dry white wine

1½ cups fresh or frozen baby fava beans

8 ounces jumbo shrimp, peeled and deveined

¼ cup chopped fresh flat-leaf parsley

salt and pepper

crusty bread, to serve

**>1** Heat the oil in a large skillet, add the scallions, and cook over medium heat, stirring occasionally, for 4–5 minutes, until soft.

**>2** Add the garlic and cook, stirring, for 30 seconds, until soft.

**>3** Add the squid and cook over high heat, stirring occasionally, for 2 minutes, or until golden brown.

**>4** Stir in the wine and bring to a boil. Add the beans, reduce the heat, cover, and simmer for 5–8 minutes, if using fresh beans, or 4–5 minutes, if using frozen beans, until tender.

**>5** Add the shrimp, re-cover, and simmer for an additional 2–3 minutes, until the shrimp turn pink and start to curl.

**>6** Stir in the parsley and season with salt and pepper. Serve hot with crusty bread to mop up the juices.

# monkfish with a lemon & parsley crust

serves 4

## ingredients

¼ cup sunflower oil

¼ cup fresh bread crumbs

¼ cup chopped fresh parsley, plus extra sprigs to garnish

finely grated rind of 1 large lemon

4 monkfish fillets, about 5–6 ounces each

salt and pepper

**>1** Preheat the oven to 350°F. Mix together the oil, bread crumbs, parsley, and lemon rind in a bowl until well combined. Season with salt and pepper.

**>2** Place the fish fillets in a large roasting pan.

**>3** Divide the bread crumb mixture among the fish and press it down with your fingers to make sure it covers the fillets.

**>4** Bake in the preheated oven for 7–8 minutes, or until the fish are cooked through. Garnish with parsley sprigs and serve.

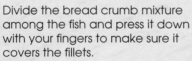

# thai shrimp noodle bowl

**serves 4**

## ingredients

1 bunch scallions
2 celery stalks
1 red bell pepper
8 ounces rice vermicelli noodles
2 tablespoons peanut oil
1/3 cup unsalted peanuts

1 fresh Thai chile, sliced
1 lemongrass stem, crushed
1¾ cups fish or chicken stock
1 cup coconut milk
2 teaspoons Thai fish sauce

12 ounces cooked, peeled
 jumbo shrimp
salt and pepper
3 tablespoons chopped fresh
 cilantro, to garnish

**>1** Trim the scallions and celery and thinly slice diagonally. Seed and thinly slice the bell pepper.

**>2** Place the noodles in a bowl, cover with boiling water, and let stand for 4 minutes, until tender, or prepare according to the package directions. Drain and set aside.

**>3** Heat the oil in a wok and stir-fry the peanuts for 1–2 minutes, until golden. Lift out with a slotted spoon.

**>4** Add the sliced vegetables to the wok and stir-fry over high heat for 1–2 minutes.

**>5** Add the chile, lemongrass, stock, coconut milk, and fish sauce and bring to a boil.

**>6** Stir in the shrimp and bring back to a boil, stirring. Season with salt and pepper, then add the noodles. Serve in warm bowls, sprinkled with chopped cilantro.

# wine-steamed mussels

**serves 4**

## ingredients

1 stick butter

1 shallot, chopped

3 garlic cloves, finely chopped

4½ pounds mussels, scrubbed
  and debearded

1 cup dry white wine

½ teaspoon salt

¼ cup chopped fresh parsley

pepper

fresh crusty bread, to serve

**>1** Place half the butter in a large saucepan and melt over low heat. Add the shallot and garlic and cook for 2 minutes.

**>2** Discard any mussels with broken shells and any that refuse to close when tapped. Add the mussels and wine to the pan and season with salt and pepper. Cover and bring to a boil, then cook for 3 minutes, shaking the pan from time to time.

**>3** Remove the mussels from the pan with a slotted spoon and place in individual serving bowls. Discard any mussels that remain closed.

**>4** Stir the remaining butter and the parsley into the cooking juices in the pan. Bring to a boil, then pour over the mussels. Serve immediately with fresh crusty bread for mopping up the juices.

# vegetarian

falafel burgers 65
mushroom & cauliflower gratin 67
jamaican rice & beans with tofu 69
broiled feta kabobs on fennel & white
   bean salad 71
tofu stir-fry 73
fusilli with zucchini & lemon 75
tomato ratatouille 77
noodle stir-fry 79
double cheese & macaroni 81
tacos with chickpea salsa 83
zucchini, carrot & tomato frittata 85
egg tortilla with feta & corn 87
goat cheese tarts 89

# falafel
# burgers

**serves 4**

## ingredients

1 (29-ounce) can chickpeas,
  drained

1 small onion, chopped

grated rind and juice of 1 lime

2 teaspoons ground coriander

2 teaspoons ground cumin

⅓ cup all-purpose flour

¼ cup olive oil

salt and pepper

4 sprigs fresh basil, to garnish

store-bought tomato salsa, to serve

**>1** Put the chickpeas, onion, lime rind and juice, and the spices into a food processor and process to a coarse paste. Season with salt and pepper.

**>2** Transfer the mixture to a clean work surface and shape into four patties.

**>3** Spread out the flour on a large plate and use to coat the patties.

**>4** Heat the oil in a large skillet, add the patties, and cook over medium heat for 2 minutes on each side, or until crisp. Garnish with basil sprigs and serve with tomato salsa.

# mushroom & cauliflower gratin

serves 4

### ingredients

1 head cauliflower, cut into florets

4 tablespoons butter

1½ cups sliced white button
  mushrooms, sliced

salt and pepper

### topping

1 cup dry bread crumbs

2 tablespoons grated Parmesan-
  style vegetarian cheese

1 teaspoon dried oregano

1 teaspoon dried parsley

2 tablespoons butter

**>1** Bring a large saucepan of lightly salted water to a boil. Add the cauliflower and cook for 3 minutes.

**>2** Remove from the heat, drain well, and transfer to a shallow ovenproof dish.

**>3** Preheat the oven to 450°F. Melt the butter in a small saucepan over medium heat. Add the mushrooms, stir, and cook gently for 3 minutes.

**>4** Remove from the heat and spoon the mushrooms on top of the cauliflower. Season with salt and pepper.

**>5** Combine the bread crumbs, Parmesan-style cheese, and herbs in a small mixing bowl, then sprinkle the mixture over the vegetables.

**>6** Dice the butter and scatter over the bread crumb mixture. Bake in the preheated oven for 15 minutes, or until the topping is golden brown. Serve straight from the cooking dish.

# jamaican rice & beans with tofu

serves 4

## ingredients

8 ounces firm tofu

2 tablespoons chopped fresh thyme, plus extra sprigs to garnish

2 tablespoons olive oil

1 onion, sliced

1 garlic clove, crushed

1 small fresh red chile, chopped

1¾ cups vegetable stock

1 cup long-grain rice

¼ cup coconut cream (from Asian grocery stores) or coconut milk

1 (15–16-ounce) can red kidney beans, rinsed and drained

salt and pepper

**>1** Cut the tofu into bite-size cubes. Toss with half the chopped thyme and season with salt and pepper.

**>2** Heat 1 tablespoon of the oil in a skillet and fry the tofu, stirring occasionally, for 2 minutes. Remove and keep warm.

**>3** Cook the onion in the remaining oil, stirring, for 3–4 minutes.

**>4** Stir in the garlic, chile, and the remaining chopped thyme, then add the stock and bring to a boil.

**>5** Stir in the rice, then reduce the heat, cover, and simmer for 12–15 minutes, until the rice is tender.

**>6** Stir in the coconut cream and beans, season with salt and pepper and cook gently for 2–3 minutes. Spoon the tofu over the rice and serve hot, garnished with thyme sprigs.

# broiled feta kabobs on fennel & white bean salad

**serves 4**

## ingredients

8 ounces feta cheese
1 garlic clove, crushed
1 fennel bulb, thinly sliced
1 small red onion, thinly sliced

1 (15–16-ounce) can cannellini
  beans, rinsed and drained
1–2 tablespoons balsamic vinegar,
  to serve

## dressing

finely grated rind and juice of
  1 lemon
3 tablespoons chopped fresh
  flat-leaf parsley
¼ cup olive oil
salt and pepper

**>1** Preheat the broiler to high. For the dressing, mix together the lemon rind and juice, parsley, and oil with salt and pepper to taste.

**>2** Cut the provolone into ¾-inch/2 cm cubes, thread onto 4 presoaked wooden skewers, and brush with the dressing.

**>3** Cook the skewers under the preheated broiler for 6–8 minutes, turning once, until golden.

**>4** Heat the remaining dressing in a small saucepan with the garlic until boiling. Combine with the fennel, onion, and beans. Serve the skewers with the salad, sprinkled with a little balsamic vinegar.

# tofu
# stir-fry
serves 4

## ingredients

2 tablespoons sunflower oil

2 cups cubed firm tofu

3 cups coarsely chopped
   bok choy

1 garlic clove, chopped

¼ cup sweet chili sauce

2 tablespoons light soy sauce

**>1** Heat 1 tablespoon of the oil in a wok.

**>2** Add the tofu to the wok in batches and stir-fry for 2–3 minutes, until golden. Remove and set aside.

**>3** Add the bok choy to the wok and stir-fry for a few seconds until tender and wilted. Remove and set aside.

**>4** Heat the remaining oil in the wok, then add the garlic and stir-fry for 30 seconds.

**>5** Stir in the chili sauce and soy sauce and bring to a boil.

**>6** Return the tofu and bok choy to the wok and toss gently until coated in the sauce. Transfer to individual dishes and serve immediately.

# fusilli with zucchini & lemon

serves 4

## ingredients

⅓ cup olive oil

1 small onion, thinly sliced

2 garlic cloves, finely chopped

2 tablespoons chopped fresh
  rosemary

1 tablespoon chopped
  fresh flat-leaf parsley

4 small zucchini, cut into
  1½-inch strips

finely grated rind of 1 lemon

1 pound dried fusilli

salt and pepper

¼ cup grated Parmesan-style
  vegetarian cheese, to serve

**>1** Heat the oil in a large skillet over medium–low heat. Add the onion and cook gently, stirring occasionally, for about 10 minutes, until golden.

**>2** Increase the heat to medium–high. Add the garlic, rosemary, and parsley. Cook for a few seconds, stirring.

**>3** Add the zucchini and lemon rind. Cook, stirring occasionally, for 5–7 minutes, until just tender. Season with salt and pepper. Remove from the heat.

**>4** Bring a large saucepan of lightly salted water to a boil. Add the pasta, bring back to a boil, and cook according to the package directions, until tender but still firm to the bite.

**>5** Drain the pasta and transfer to a warm serving dish.

**>6** Briefly reheat the zucchini sauce. Pour over the pasta and toss well to mix. Sprinkle with the Parmesan-style cheese and serve immediately.

# tomato ratatouille

**serves 4**

## ingredients

1 teaspoon olive oil

1 onion, cut into small wedges

2–4 garlic cloves, chopped

1 small eggplant, chopped

1 red and 1 yellow bell pepper,
  seeded and chopped

1 zucchini, chopped

2 tablespoons tomato paste

3 tablespoons water

1½ cups halved white button
  mushrooms,

2 tomatoes, chopped

pepper

1 tablespoon chopped fresh basil,
  to garnish

2 tablespoons grated Parmesan-
  style vegetarian cheese, to serve

**>1** Heat the oil in a heavy saucepan. Add the onion, garlic, and eggplant and cook, stirring frequently, for 3 minutes.

**>2** Add the red and yellow bell peppers and the zucchini.

**>3** Mix together the tomato paste and water in a small bowl and stir into the pan. Bring to a boil, cover, reduce the heat to a simmer, and cook for 10 minutes.

**>4** Add the mushrooms and tomatoes, season with pepper, and continue to simmer for 12–15 minutes, stirring occasionally, until the vegetables are tender. Divide the ratatouille among warm dishes, garnish with chopped basil, and serve with Parmesan-style cheese.

# noodle stir-fry

**serves 2**

## ingredients

4 ounces flat rice noodles
⅓ cup soy sauce
2 tablespoons lemon juice
1 teaspoon sugar
½ teaspoon cornstarch

1 tablespoon vegetable oil
2 teaspoons grated fresh ginger
2 garlic cloves, chopped
4–5 scallions, trimmed and sliced

2 tablespoons rice wine or
dry sherry
1 (8-ounce) can water chestnuts,
drained and sliced

**>1** Put the noodles in a bowl with boiling water for 4 minutes, or prepare according to the package directions. Drain and rinse under cold water.

**>2** Mix together the soy sauce, lemon juice, sugar, and cornstarch in a small bowl. Set aside.

**>3** Heat the oil in a wok, add the ginger and garlic, and stir-fry for 1 minute.

**>4** Add the scallions and stir-fry for 3 minutes.

**>5** Add the rice wine, then add the soy sauce mixture and cook for 1 minute.

**>6** Stir in the water chestnuts and noodles and cook for an additional 1–2 minutes, or until heated through. Transfer to individual dishes and serve immediately.

# double cheese & macaroni

serves 4

## ingredients

8 ounces dried macaroni

8 ounces ricotta cheese

1½ tablespoons whole-grain mustard

3 tablespoons snipped fresh chives, plus extra to garnish

12 cherry tomatoes, halved

⅔ cup drained and chopped sun-dried tomatoes in oil

butter or oil, for greasing

1 cup shredded cheddar cheese

salt and pepper

Bring a large saucepan of lightly salted water to a boil. Add the macaroni and cook according to the package directions, until tender but still firm to the bite. Remove from the heat and drain well.

Mix the ricotta with the mustard and chives and season with salt and pepper. Stir in the macaroni, cherry tomatoes, and sun-dried tomatoes.

Grease a 1¾-quart, shallow ovenproof dish. Spoon in the macaroni mixture, spreading it evenly.

Preheat the broiler to high. Sprinkle the cheddar cheese over the macaroni mixture and cook under the preheated broiler for 4–5 minutes, until golden and bubbling. Serve the macaroni sprinkled with snipped chives.

# tacos with chickpea salsa

serves 4

## ingredients

2 firm, ripe avocados

1 tablespoon lime juice

1 tomato, diced

1 tablespoon olive oil

1 small onion, sliced

1 (15–16-ounce) can chickpeas, drained

1 teaspoon mild chili powder

8 romaine lettuce leaves

8 tacos

2 tablespoons chopped fresh cilantro, plus extra sprigs to garnish

salt and pepper

⅔ cup sour cream, to serve

**>1** Halve, pit, peel, and dice the avocados and toss with the lime juice.

**>2** Stir in the tomato and season well with salt and pepper.

**>3** Heat the oil in a saucepan and sauté the onion for 3–4 minutes, or until golden brown.

**>4** Mash the chickpeas with a fork and stir into the pan with the chili powder. Heat gently, stirring, for 2 minutes.

**>5** Divide the lettuce among the tacos. Stir the chopped cilantro into the avocado-and-tomato mixture, then spoon into the tortillas.

**>6** Add a spoonful of the chickpea mixture to each taco and top with a spoonful of sour cream. Garnish with cilantro sprigs and serve immediately.

# zucchini, carrot & tomato frittata

serves 2–4

### ingredients

1 teaspoon olive oil

1 onion, cut into small wedges

1–2 garlic cloves, crushed

2 eggs

2 egg whites

1 zucchini, trimmed and grated

2 carrots, peeled and grated

2 tomatoes, chopped

pepper

1 tablespoon chopped fresh basil, to garnish

**>1** Heat the oil in a large, nonstick skillet, add the onion and garlic, and sauté for 5 minutes, stirring frequently.

**>2** Beat together the eggs and egg whites in a bowl, then pour into the skillet.

**>3** Using a spatula, pull the egg mixture from the sides of the skillet into the center, letting the uncooked egg run underneath.

**>4** When the bottom has set lightly, add the zucchini, carrots, and tomatoes. Season with pepper and continue to cook over low heat until the eggs are cooked to your liking. Sprinkle with the chopped basil, cut the frittata into quarters, and serve.

# egg tortilla with feta & corn

**serves 2**

## ingredients

3 potatoes
2 tablespoons olive oil
1 onion, chopped
1 zucchini, coarsely grated
1¼ cups of drained, canned
   corn kernels

6 eggs
⅔ cup drained and crumbled
   feta cheese
salt and pepper
paprika, for sprinkling

**>1** Peel or scrub the potatoes and cut into ½-inch dice.

**>2** Cook the potatoes in a saucepan of lightly salted boiling water for 5 minutes, or until just tender. Drain.

**>3** Heat the oil in a large ovenproof skillet over medium heat and sauté the onion for about 5 minutes, or until softened. Stir in the zucchini and potatoes, then cook for 2 minutes. Stir in the corn kernels.

**>4** Season the eggs with salt and pepper and beat lightly. Meanwhile, preheat the broiler to high.

**>5** Stir the eggs into the skillet, then scatter the feta cheese over the eggs. Cook for 4–6 minutes, until almost set. Place the tortilla under the preheated broiler for 2–3 minutes, until set and golden brown.

**>6** Sprinkle the tortilla with paprika and cut into 4–6 wedges. Serve the tortilla hot or cold.

# goat cheese tarts

makes 12 tarts

## ingredients

melted butter, for greasing
1 sheet ready-to-bake puff pastry
flour, for dusting
1 egg, beaten

about ¼ cup onion relish or
    tomato relish
12 ounces goat cheese logs,
    sliced into 12 circles

olive oil, for drizzling
pepper

**>1** Preheat the oven to 400°F. Grease two baking sheets with melted butter.

**>2** Transfer the pastry sheet to a lightly floured surface and roll out lightly to remove any creases, if necessary. Use a 3-inch pastry cutter to stamp out 12 circles.

**>3** Place the circles on the baking sheets and press gently about 1 inch from the edge of each with a 2-inch pastry cutter. Brush with the beaten egg and prick with a fork.

**>4** Top each circle with a teaspoon of the relish and a slice of the goat cheese.

**>5** Drizzle the oil over the tarts and sprinkle with a little black pepper.

**>6** Bake in the preheated oven for 8–10 minutes, or until the pastry is crisp and the cheese is bubbling. Serve warm.

# desserts

# quick tiramisu

serves 4

## ingredients

1 cup mascarpone cheese

1 egg, separated

2 tablespoons plain yogurt

2 tablespoons sugar

2 tablespoons dark rum

2 tablespoons cold, strong black coffee

8 ladyfingers

2 tablespoons grated semisweet dark chocolate

**>1** Mix together the mascarpone cheese, egg yolk, and yogurt in a large bowl. Beat until smooth.

**>2** Whip the egg white in a separate bowl until stiff but not dry. Add the sugar and gently fold into the mascarpone mixture. Divide half the mixture among four sundae glasses.

**>3** Mix together the rum and coffee in a shallow dish.

**>4** Dip the ladyfingers into the rum mixture, break them into small pieces, and divide among the glasses.

**>5** Stir any remaining coffee mixture into the remaining mascarpone mixture and divide among the glasses.

**>6** Sprinkle with grated chocolate. Serve immediately or cover and chill until required.

# caramel pecan apples

serves 4

## ingredients

4 tablespoons unsalted butter

¼ cup packed light brown sugar

4 crisp apples, such as McIntosh or Pippin, cored and cut into wedges

1 teaspoon ground cinnamon

4 thick slices of brioche

¼ cup rum or apple juice

⅓ cup pecans

>**1** Melt the butter in a sauté pan and stir in the sugar, apples, and cinnamon.

>**2** Cook over medium heat, stirring occasionally, for 5–6 minutes, until caramelized and golden.

>**3** Meanwhile, toast the brioche on both sides until golden.

>**4** Stir the rum and pecans into the pan and cook for an additional minute. Spoon the apple mixture over the toasted brioche and serve immediately.

# blueberry & amaretti with yogurt

serves 4

## ingredients

1¾ cups fresh blueberries

1 teaspoon almond extract

3 tablespoons honey

16 amaretti cookies, plus extra
 to serve

1¾ cups Greek-style yogurt

**>1** Place 1½ cups of the blueberries in a bowl with the almond extract and 1 tablespoon of the honey. Mash lightly with a fork.

**>2** Crumble the amaretti cookies with your fingers to break up coarsely.

**>3** Lightly stir together the mashed berries, cookies, and yogurt, then spoon into four small glasses or dishes.

**>4** Top each glass with the remaining blueberries and drizzle the remaining honey over them. Serve with extra amaretti cookies on the side.

# plum & almond wraps

**makes 4 wraps**

## ingredients

1 sheet ready-to-bake puff pastry

⅓ cup almond meal
  (ground almonds)

2½ tablespoons sugar

½ teaspoon ground star anise

4 red plums

milk, for glazing

**>1** Preheat the oven to 425°F. Line a baking sheet with parchment paper. Cut the pastry into four equal rectangles.

**>2** Stir together the almond meal, sugar, and star anise, then place a tablespoonful in the center of each pastry rectangle.

**>3** Halve and pit the plums and cut each into 8 slices.

**>4** Arrange the plum slices diagonally across the middle of each pastry rectangle, over the almond mix.

**>5** Sprinkle any remaining almond mix over the top, then fold two opposite corners of each pastry rectangle over to enclose the plum slices, securing with milk.

**>6** Lift onto the baking sheet and brush with milk to glaze. Bake in the preheated oven for 15–20 minutes, until crisp and golden. Serve warm.

# pear & hazelnut crepes

**serves 4**

## ingredients

1 cup chocolate hazelnut spread

8 crepes (made from a pancake mix, adding extra milk so the batter is runny—look for directions on the package)

4 ripe pears

3 tablespoons unsalted butter, melted

2 tablespoons demerara sugar or other raw sugar

⅓ cup toasted hazelnuts, chopped, to serve

> **>1** Preheat the broiler to high. Warm the chocolate spread gently in a small saucepan until softened.

> **>2** Using a spatula, spread each crepe with a little of the warm chocolate spread.

> **>3** Peel, core, and chop the pears. Arrange the pears over the chocolate spread, then bring the opposite sides of the crepes over the filling to enclose it.

> **>4** Lightly brush an ovenproof dish with a little of the melted butter.

> **>5** Arrange the crepes in the dish. Brush the crepes with the remaining melted butter and sprinkle with the demerara sugar.

> **>6** Place the dish under the preheated broiler and cook for 4–5 minutes, until bubbling and lightly browned. Scatter the toasted hazelnuts over the crepes and serve hot.

# no-bake chocolate fudge cake

**serves 12**

## ingredients

8 ounces semisweet dark
 chocolate, broken into pieces
2 sticks unsalted butter
3 tablespoons black coffee

¼ cup packed light brown sugar
vanilla extract
3 cups crushed graham crackers

½ cup raisins
⅔ cup chopped walnuts

Line the bottom and sides of an 8-inch cake pan with parchment paper.

Melt the chocolate and butter with the coffee, sugar, and a few drops of vanilla extract in a saucepan over low heat.

**>3**

Stir in the crushed crackers, raisins, and walnuts and stir well.

**>4**

Spoon the mixture into the prepared cake pan. Transfer to the refrigerator and let set for 1–2 hours. Invert and cut into thin slices to serve.

# warm honey muffins with strawberry salsa

**serves 6**

## ingredients

butter or oil, for greasing
1 ⅓ cups all-purpose flour
2 teaspoons baking powder
1 teaspoon baking soda
¼ cup honey
3 tablespoons light brown sugar

4 tablespoons unsalted butter, melted
1 egg, beaten
⅓ cup Greek-style yogurt
finely grated rind of 1 small orange
warmed honey, to glaze

## salsa

8 oz fresh strawberries
2 tablespoons honey
2 tablespoons orange juice

**>1** Preheat the oven to 400°F. Lightly grease six individual metal moulds or six cups in a deep muffin pan.

**>2** Sift the flour, baking powder, and baking soda into a bowl and add the honey, sugar, butter, egg, yogurt, and orange rind, mixing lightly.

**>3** Spoon the batter into the molds and bake in the preheated oven for about 20 minutes, until well risen and firm.

**>4** Meanwhile, for the salsa, hull and coarsely chop the strawberries.

**>5** Warm the honey and orange juice in a small saucepan, without boiling, then pour over the strawberries and stir lightly.

**>6** Remove the muffins from the oven, lift carefully from the molds, and brush the tops with honey to glaze. Serve the muffins on warm serving plates with a spoonful of strawberry salsa on the side.

# white wine & honey syllabub

**serves 4**

## ingredients

3 tablespoons brandy

3 tablespoons white wine

2½ cups heavy cream

⅓ cup honey

½ cup slivered almonds

**>1** Combine the brandy and wine in a bowl.

**>2** Pour the cream into a large bowl and whisk until just thickened.

**>3** Add the honey to the cream and whisk for about 15 seconds.

**>4** Pour the brandy and wine mixture in a continuous stream into the cream and honey mixture, whisking continuously, until the mixture forms soft peaks.

**>5** Spoon into serving dishes.

**>6** Transfer to the refrigerator and let chill for 2–3 hours. Scatter the slivered almonds over the syllabubs and serve.

# chocolate & orange desserts

**serves 4**

## ingredients

1 orange

4 ounces semisweet dark
  chocolate, broken into pieces

2 tablespoons unsalted butter

3 tablespoons maple syrup

1 tablespoon orange liqueur

½ cup crème fraîche

strips of orange zest, to decorate

>1 Cut the white pith and peel from the orange and lift out the segments, catching the juices in a bowl. Cut the segments into small chunks.

>2 Place the chocolate, butter, maple syrup, and liqueur in a small saucepan with the reserved orange juice and heat gently, stirring, until smooth.

>3 Stir in ¼ cup of the crème fraîche and the orange chunks.

>4 Spoon the mixture into four serving dishes, then top each with a spoonful of the remaining crème fraîche. Scatter the strips of orange zest over the top to decorate.

# brown sugar mocha cream desserts

serves 4

## ingredients

1¼ cups heavy cream

1 teaspoon vanilla extract

2 cups fresh whole-wheat bread crumbs

⅓ cup packed dark brown sugar

1 tablespoon instant coffee granules

2 tablespoons unsweetened cocoa powder

grated chocolate, to decorate (optional)

**>1** Whisk together the cream and vanilla extract in a large bowl until thick and holding soft peaks.

**>2** Mix together the bread crumbs, sugar, coffee, and cocoa powder in a separate large bowl.

**>3** Layer the bread crumb mixture with the cream in serving glasses, finishing with a layer of cream. Sprinkle with the grated chocolate, if using.

**>4** Cover with plastic wrap and chill in the refrigerator for several hours, or overnight.

# butterscotch, mango & ginger sundaes

serves 4

## ingredients

½ cup packed light brown sugar
½ cup light corn syrup
4 tablespoons unsalted butter

½ cup heavy cream
½ teaspoon vanilla extract
1 large, ripe mango
16 gingersnaps

2 pints vanilla ice cream
2 tablespoons coarsely chopped
  almonds, toasted

**>1** To make the butterscotch sauce, melt the brown sugar, corn syrup, and butter in a small saucepan and simmer for 3 minutes, stirring, until smooth.

**>2** Stir in the cream and vanilla extract, then remove from the heat.

**>3** Peel and pit the mango and cut into ½-inch cubes.

**>4** Place the gingersnaps in a plastic food bag and crush lightly with a rolling pin.

**>5** Divide half the mango among four glasses and top each with a scoop of the ice cream.

**>6** Spoon over a little butterscotch sauce and sprinkle with the crushed gingersnaps. Repeat with the remaining ingredients. Sprinkle some of the almonds over the top of each sundae and serve immediately.

# raspberry & croissant desserts

**serves 4**

## ingredients

2 tablespoons unsalted butter, melted

4 croissants

1¾ cups fresh raspberries

¼ cup maple syrup

1½ cups milk

2 extra-large eggs, beaten

1 teaspoon vanilla extract

freshly grated nutmeg, to taste

**>1** Preheat the oven to 425°F. Place a baking sheet on the middle shelf.

**>2** Brush four 1½-cup ramekins (individual ceramic dishes) or custard cups with half the butter.

**>3** Chop the croissants into bite-size chunks. Mix with the raspberries and divide among the dishes. Spoon 1 tablespoon of the maple syrup over the contents of each dish.

**>4** Heat the milk until almost boiling, then quickly beat in the eggs and vanilla extract. Pour the milk mixture evenly over the dishes, pressing the croissants down lightly.

**>5** Drizzle with the remaining butter and sprinkle a little nutmeg over each dish.

**>6** Place the dishes on the baking sheet and bake in the preheated oven for about 20 minutes, until lightly set. Serve hot.

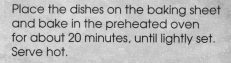

# brandy snaps

makes 20–30 brandy snaps

## ingredients

6 tablespoons unsalted butter

⅓ cup sugar

3 tablespoons light corn syrup

⅔ cup all-purpose flour

1 teaspoon ground ginger

1 tablespoon brandy

finely grated rind of ½ lemon

## filling

⅔ cup heavy cream

1 tablespoon brandy (optional)

1 tablespoon confectioners' sugar

**>1** Preheat the oven to 325°F. Line three baking sheets with parchment paper.

**>2** Place the butter, sugar, and corn syrup in a saucepan and heat gently over low heat, stirring occasionally until smooth. Remove from the heat and let cool slightly.

**>3** Sift the flour and ginger into the pan and beat until smooth, then stir in the brandy and lemon rind. Drop small spoonfuls of the mixture onto the baking sheets, allowing plenty of space for spreading.

**>4** Place one baking sheet at a time in the preheated oven for 10–12 minutes, or until the snaps are golden brown.

**>5** Remove the first baking sheet from the oven. Let cool for about 30 seconds, then lift each snap with a spatula and wrap around the handle of a wooden spoon to shape it. If the snaps become too firm, return to the oven for about 30 seconds to soften.

**>6** Transfer the snaps to a wire rack to cool. Repeat with the remaining snaps, one baking sheet at a time. For the filling, combine all the ingredients and whip until thick. Pipe into both ends of each brandy snap and serve immediately.